PARENTS
CAN.LIVE

ELIZABETH WILEY MA JD, POMO ELDER

Order this book online at www.trafford.com
or email orders@trafford.com

Most Trafford titles are also available at major online book retailers.

 www.trafford.com

North America & international
toll-free: 844 688 6899 (USA & Canada)
fax: 812 355 4082

Our mission is to efficiently provide the world's finest, most comprehensive book publishing
service, enabling every author to experience success. To find out how to publish your book,
your way, and have it available worldwide, visit us online at www.trafford.com

ISBN: 978-1-6987-1035-8 (sc)
ISBN: 978-1-6987-1036-5 (e)

Print information available on the last page.

Trafford rev. 11/26/2021

Parents CAN either live, or be alive, surviving and often suffering….as YOU read and interpret the title of this series and this book, you CAN figure it out for YOUR life.

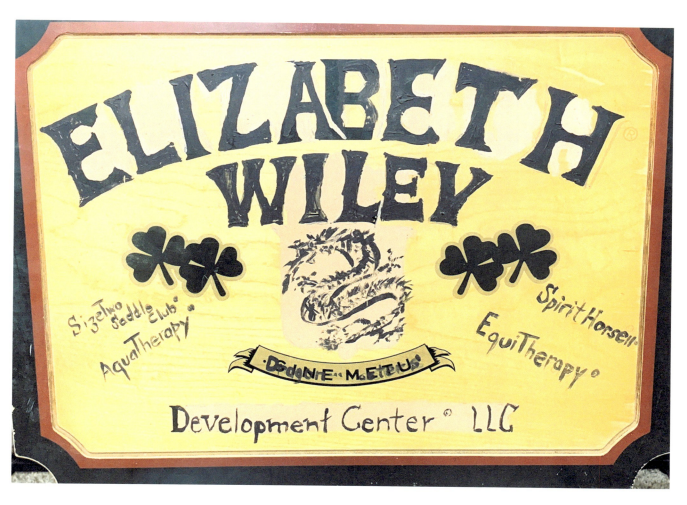

OUR TEACHING WORKBOOK SERIES

Introduction:

Our books are written as on ongoing series for high risk youth, veterans, and first responders as well as their parents and those who are raising them.

One of the reasons for starting this series was we, as special needs teachers, as therapists, as Directors of programs and private schools for high risk youth began to recognize how many of the children and youth were children of veterans, grandchildren of veterans, and also first responders.

We then noticed the numbers of minority children and poverty level financial back grounds were the reality for high risk children and youth.

We saw children of Mothers who had been as young as NINE at the birth of their child among the high risk students. Whether rich, or poverty level, we saw children of alcohol, sexual, and drug addictions.

We saw children as young as 18 months labeled with an alphabet of mental health disorders, medicated and put into "special schools" where in fact media found they were often warehoused, abused, and not taught at all. Upon seeing a news story about the schools discovered at some of the licensed sites, in which children and teens often did not have desks, or chairs to sit on, let alone proper educational supplies and equipment for special learning program, we joined with others, and designed programs.

We were naive enough to think our work, offered FREE in most cases, would be welcomed especially as we offer it free and often through research projects, but, it was NOT valued or wanted.

What? we asked?

We went back to college and while earning degrees we had apparently NOT needed while working with children of the very rich in expensive private schools, we did research projects to document our findings. To find ways to overcome the problems. Again, our work was NOT valued or wanted.

One of our associates, who had asked many of us to volunteer in a once a month FREE reading program in the local public schools, was held back for almost two years doing paperwork and proving her volunteers, most of them parents of successful children, teens and adults, could read a first five years book and teach parents how to read those books to their own children. She was a Deputy United States Prosecutor, and had recruited friends from all levels of law enforcement, child and family services, education and volunteer groups that served children and families.

None the less, we continued our work, met a fabulous and expensive Psychiatrist who was building his own server system and the first online education project after creating a massive and encompassing medical examination study guide for graduate medical students to assist them in passing global and national medical examinations for licensing.

We worked with a team of citizens and specialists in education who had created a 39 manual project for students, parents and teachers to be able to learn on their own.

This series of books includes ideas, history and thoughts from the students, the parents, and professionals who work with these situations.

Jesus was told, don't have children wasting your time, and he responded, let the children come.

Our work is to bring children to us, and to those who have the heart and love to develop the uniqueness and individuality of each of God's creations. Many of them are of different religions, and beliefs, and many are atheists but believe fully in the wonder and uniqueness of every human.

To all who have helped and continue to help children and anyone wanting to learn, we thank God and we thank you.

PARENTS are the most important ingredient in a child learning to live successfully and happily to find their own purpose and dream and meet that vision.

PARENTS have often been broken by their own parents, teachers, and counselors who were SUPPOSED to have helped them develop.

Blaming parents, grandparents, foster parents, or group homes and teachers is NOT going to help you, or your child.

The exercises in this book are easy. This book is not written for academic stars, it is written for parents, from nine (YES, there are nine year old parents in America and around the world today)to seventy (people who did not consider that growing up without a parent for love and support was not an important thought for any child of theirs) who have decided to give their child the BEST possible support for a happy childhood, and a successful adulthood.

WHAT IS MY DREAM?

FOR ME.....

Introductory Chapter by Elizabeth Wiley MA JD, Native California POMO, Elder

Once there was an Oprah Winfrey show in which people discussed what they had made out of old cardboard boxes and what they had dreamed for their lives. One amazing astronaut told of his sitting in the backyard of his home, family and friends laughing at him, or saying with a discounting "how cute" while he created his cardboard spaceships, he dreamed of being the first man on the moon. He was.

Another woman was very successful, but very unhappy. When she was asked to do the cardboard box exercise, she sat in the empty box and went back to her childhood of wanting to be a police officer. Instead she did what was sensible, got a good education, a good job, married a good provider and felt deeply unhappy.

Over the years we have gotten out the cardboard boxes, construction paper, tape, and scissors and crayons with adults and children alike, and asked them to make their dreams.........then started working on making those dreams a reality.

You might say, I am forty-five, am one hundred pounds overweight, and my dream was to be a dancer.

Sit in that box, put that box in front of your refrigerator. Your children will love it.

Take a selfie of yourself in that decorated box, and take it shopping with you. Your children will probably NOT like it when you say, if you want treats, you have to earn money to buy them, and ask for special treat meals for the whole family, but I can not have all this fattening food around me all the time.

YOUR dreams as a parent are important. Making your childhood ideas of what YOU wanted to be given to you, as a child, to your child, is NOT the same as making your own dreams come true. Their dreams are NOT your old unmet dreams.

Are you going to be the most famous dancer ever? Who knows, a quiet little woman came into the camera on a televised international talent show......most people had no clue, then she began to sing......everyone has heard Susan Boyle and loves her music, and her inspiration.

BUT, *you might become a dance teacher and dance, learn how to create stage settings, and get parent volunteers who also have unmet dreams. You might be THE teacher and inspiration for a very famous dancer. Martha Graham was one of the most famous dance teachers ever, when she had a stroke, she forced herself to do her Barre exercises everyday and recovered. She was often featured in talks to disabled dancers, and to stroke victims to rebuild their lives.*

AND *we all need to remind ourselves that dreams can change, or be adjusted. Two sons of a friend were in bands, and doing really well in high school. Then they were invited to backstage of the US Festival, and realized they liked playing music with friends, in parties and back yards, and small clubs, but did NOT like the fame and fortune scene they witnessed at that concert. Both have had great careers and lives, not at all wondering if they "should" have gone a different path.*

PARENTS CAN LIVE

Parents need to understand that their life is not OVER because they somehow "got" stuck with children.

When Parents LIVE their own lives, they pass along joy, enthusiasm and inspire their children to set goals, and learn how to reach those goals. The children watch their parents ask professionals for help, read books and find online help to reach their goals.

Children who grow up with even one adult who encourages them by living their own dreams are much more likely to grow up happy, enthusiastic and able to find and meet their own life goals.

Children who grow up with even ONE adult who lives a realistic balanced life will have a better chance to grow up themselves into realistic balanced lives.

Tee shirts we designed for 5 year global spay and neuter million more spay project for OUR Community ROOTS AND SHOOTS PROJECT (you can start your own local environmental)

CHAPTER ONE

Before Birth

While most parents reading this book will already have children, they may have other, older children, or they may be doing research into how to raise their newest child in a more balanced, joyfilled, and successful way than they were raised. This is not to blame grandparents, or great - grandparents or society for the problems so you are not responsible for raising your own child in a positive way for a happy life.

As you read the Chapter below on owning pets, you too need to be prepared for having children. They are not "accidents", or something you "got" because you were drunk, or loaded, or unprepared. Read the chapter on sex, and stop blaming anyone but yourself for unwanted children.

Children are an amazing gift. We need to treat them as such.

If someone gave you a super expensive sports car, how would you treat it???

Look at the car you have today, you would probably treat it the same way, filled with cans and fast food wrappers, food and drink splashed around, Tires paper thin because paying those registration costs, and those oil, lube and service costs are as high every few months. as the down payment on a new car. Especially if you have purchased a high cost maintenance used car. Read the Chapter on Finance, and training children about successful financial success in the real world.

Be honest about how you treat your relatives, your friends, your pets, your house plants, your house, your car, your clothing. You can NOT just toss your child to the thrift shop if that child is not what the trendy child of the moment looks like.

If you have not had pets, as a grown up, and taken proper care of them, you need to before thinking about having a child. A baby is not a pretty picture on the mantel, it is not videos of all the lavish parties you give for your long past child who wanted them. Foster some pets for a rescue before you attempt to own one yourself. Volunteer in pre-schools and children programs at zoos, and museums before you begin to think of having a baby. Volunteer to raise money for children's hospitals, and for children's research hospitals. Volunteer in foster group homes, and probation programs. Be prepared for your own life, and help others deal with some of the realities of childhood.

Prepare yourself to be a parent, or for the new child by becoming prepared to be a good parent. Your other children will benefit as well.

BABY SHOWERS

Baby showers at one time were a time to bless the Mother and child for safe birthing and to give gifts to the Mother to help with raising the child, and gifts to the child for a happy and successful life. Today that often means starting a college savings account at your credit union or bank for the unborn child. It often means bring books and other items (you CAN register these educational gifts and tell people which stores have your registration lists, or you CAN send out a daily update on what gifts are already purchased by relatives and friends. While the lovely clothes, and cute baby items are to be encouraged, let them be attached to the educational gifts, and cash cards for the college account. Some great gifts are a world map, a national map, a state map, both for the wall, and for pre-school age children, and a globe. NASA and others sites often feature maps of the galaxy, the universe, and have ongoing video online of the ongoing learning from the space cameras that send back new learning about the universe, everyday.

PRENATAL CARE

There are way too many women today who want to attack anyone they can corner with the story that they had a seven pound baby, and only gained five pounds. Ask your child, who has bad teeth, bad bones, and maybe juvenile diabetes how great that was for the baby that attempted to grow in starvation conditions. When you develop serious health problems later in life because the fetus was feeding off your bones and muscles tissue during its critical formation stage, you will STOP raving about your wonderful accomplishment.

GET A SERIOUS nutritionist, that has your same goal, healthy happy baby that can grow into a happy healthy adult, and happy, healthy you. DO NOT listen to your Mom, who thinks you are (on the other side of the scale) too thin, and should "eat for two. You will be very sad to have your seven pound baby and find that other eighty five pounds is lovely fat attached to YOU.

GET into a serious prenatal care program to have help from other mothers. YES, it is hard to go nine months without some of the things you think you can NOT live without, your child is going to be grateful to have a healthy start for bones, teeth, brain and all organs.

Hopefully you have gotten into a relationship class and figured out what YOU need in a relationship and how to find the right relationship BEFORE getting pregnant. IF not, hopefully BOTH of you will get into a class and figure out how best to parent your child, even if it means to split up BEFORE the child is born, and spend all that money and drama time on raising a great child, instead of playing games, and harming everyone.

PRENATAL CARE. TAKE CARE OF YOU

SLEEP

Take a sleep class if necessary. Learn that certain hours are for sleeping. A certain place is for sleeping, and that YOU need a certain amount of sleep. Your baby is very likely to get into YOUR rhythm BEFORE being born, and you will have a lot less of those sleepless nights from new parenting.

TAKE A CHILDCARE CLASS

BOTH OF YOU.

Take a class that trains you how to make sure your baby has the best chance to fit seamlessly into YOUR life, rather than how to figure out nine thousand and ten ways to make your own life stressed and in the doing so, making your child incapable of learning how to deal in the real world. You will end up resenting and hating your baby, your baby will feel unloved and resented. The classes are well worth it. Just be sure the class is YOUR lifestyle, not trying to fit you into someone else's idea of what good parenting is.

If one or both of you rides motorcycles, and likes to work on them in the garage with the radio or cable radio blaring at top volume, do NOT bother to go to a class that tells you to get ocean and raindrop sound tapes, and make sure you buy booties for the cats and dogs so their toenails do not click on the floor.

Children adjust, and if they spent nine months before birth hearing motorcycles roar, and music blare, they will already be ready for it when they are born. And YOU are not going to feel left out sitting home with your soft tapes and drawn shades.

BLANKETS and clothing. People who had a Grandmother from a snow ridden state can be seen on any street or in any mall parking lot with a poor baby bundled up in blankets, and clothing in triple digit sunny areas of the world. IF YOU are wearing shorts, and sandals, or a sun dress and flip flops, do NOT dress your child as your Grandmother warns you is necessary. This is a good lesson to learn for your child's state of mind, and your own. Learn to stop listening to those old tapes of "wear a jacket", "wear long pants", or whatever those old cold weather people want. Put a coat and jacket stand near the door. If YOU feel cold, wear a jacket, and take a blanket for your baby. IF NOT. Do NOT swaddle that poor baby in clothing for Alaskan winters, and do NOT cover them in thick blankets. Get strollers with a sunshade, and AIR FLOW.

It is unsafe to leave babies in HOT cars, houses, or strollers with hot blankets over them. Your child can DIE, or have serious neurological damage. On the same note, just because you were a surf kid from a year round sunshine state, do NOT let your poor baby get frost bite because you do not think about cold feet, or needing a sweater or coat or mittens. Babies can also die from the cold, or lose fingers and toes to frost bite.

The classes help you both adjust to what YOU need and what YOUR baby needs instead of what your Mom, his Mom, and all the grandparents and relatives and friends tell you to do.

CHAPTER TWO

Birth to Age One

IF there is one thing to stress, it is that your child is NOT going to get a scholarship and suddenly learn to love education, or learn to want to catch up with the students who HAVE learned science, technology, education, art, and math and how to be successful and happy the day they arrive at college.

GET YOURSELF up to speed. LOVE education. Dr. David Hall, MD PhD, the Founder of fwu.org, the first electronic factoid units (NOT electronic flashcards) and a system to help a student, teacher or parent find out what building blocks of education are MISSING and fill them in, said, education is setting a fire, not filling a bucket. If your child sees you enjoy learning, your child is going to learn to love learning. If you force facts into your child and expect that child to vomit them back consistently to get good grades, you are going to make sure your child does NOT love learning, which is necessary for any goal that requires learning.

Starting with the youngest toddlers each of us can add the tinder, give the kindling, add the logs that will be there when a child begins to burn to learn. AND by forcing, pushing, and demanding too much of our child, we can make sure they do NOT love learning, and do NOT form their own dreams. It is a delicate balance of our own needs, and those of a child who we are gifted with.

There is an amazing book, TA for TODDLERS which helps a parent to learn how to help themselves let their own inner child grow and to help their baby grow into a balanced child that is neither selfish or self demeaning. TA is a therapy modality called transactional analysis that has the premise that YOU are OK, and I am OK and together we can have a wonderful world.

THIS DOES NOT MEAN answer insistent and soul crushing "WHY" questions.

Instead, build a "how to answer" the question for themselves system to teach them.

The Bible itself says as the twig is bent, so grows the tree. In educating your child, this means, do NOT create a child who pesters with a question "why" when in fact it is more than generally a delaying manipulation than a wonder at life.

This is the time to teach your child that a computer or tablet, or phone is to help us learn, to be part of society, NOT a way to hide from reality of real relationships, or to cause accidents, or get hit by cars or other persons walking down the streets and hallways with our eyes glues to a screen. Teach your child, when they ask "WHY" how to find the answer, at this point with your help, and as time goes on, by themselves. TEACH them how to find an answer online, then to go to the library and find books beyond those on online book sites, and how to find people who are experts in the answer to the question and to find their answers for the questions.

Many an auto insurance commercial or ad has been based on the real sad statistics of the numbers of youth with new driver's licenses who die, or kill and maim others for that hot question. WHEREUAT? or WHZUP? Most police and paramedics do not need the amount of online time they utilize, no other drivers need it at all. Teach your children to have a passenger take video or pictures, NOT try to take it themselves while driving. Teach your children to learn the voice activated note taking service in their phones and cars to save questions and thoughts for later when NOT driving. This starts as YOU do this when your baby is in the car with you and other driving adults.

What YOU do in these formative earliest years will train your child what kind of person and what kind of learner to become.

RACISM, CLASSISM, GENDER BIAS

This early age is where your child is picking up unspoken feelings and body language from you. It is the time when your child learns what you are subconsciously teaching them about your own insecurities and bias that have more than likely held you back in your own life.

CHAPTER THREE

Age One to Three

In the years between. one and three, your child is learning a lot more than you might think. If your family speaks two or more languages, this is the time to have the child around grandparents, and other relatives who speak the language of that part of the family. This is discussed further in the later Chapter discussing Racism, Classism, and Gender bias.

CHAPTER FOUR

Age Four

Four is the year your child truly starts to know they are they, and you are you. A child at this age learns to apply the concept "MINE' and to accept what is "yours" IF you make this a calm transition with respect for each other.

This is the time for YOU to make sure family of all ages are on the same page about these and other issues regarding personal respect, and yet, self discipline and the need for a child to get going in a balance between self and society.

In the year your child is four, your child is more than likely going to be in a pre-school, or interviewing for a private pre-school. IF your child does not know the things contained in this chapter, they are very likely to be sent to a therapist and labeled some kind of developmentally disabled, and/or put on medication at this early age. Sadly many of the children so labeled and harmed in their small lives are really not knowing of the following important realities.

YOU do NOT own the whole world.

THE world expects YOU to live by some rules.

The Catch 22 (read the book, or look up the definition in an American language dictionary after the seventies) is that it is the parent's job to at the same time to teach the child to BE themselves, and honor that self-ness, while honoring and respecting the selfness of everyone else.

CHAPTER FIVE

Age Five

The age of five in America is usually kindergarten. For many families this is the first time their child goes off alone. For others, the children have been going to childcare while parents worked, and/or to pre-school to learn how to NOT flunk kindergarten, or even worse, fail the interviews to get into a good kindergarten. A good kindergarten is one in which the child is going to learn what is needed to pass the interviews and tests for private schools, and for the higher level classes and programs in public schools.

HOW CAN A CHILD FLUNK KINDERGARTEN INTERVIEWS????

As noted above in children who can and daily DO fail pre-school, and pre-school admission interviews and testing, your child can start life very sadly as a kindergarten failure if YOU have failed to prepare them for the interview and testing by LIVING a life that leads them to be successful.

As noted in the Chapter on ages three and four, a. child going into kindergarten is expected to have skills and reading readiness and math readiness. If your child does not have these skills and readiness experiences, the child is going to fail, and / or not be allowed into a high level kindergarten.

This is NOT about whether you have pushed your child to read at a college level, or even know the entire alphabet, but in todays world, you child needs to know many skills.

One of the most important skills is the ability to get along with other children and to respect the authority of the teachers. You have (or have not) taught these skills by your own interactions with others, in your family, on your block, in the stores, and on the streets. You have taught (or NOT) these skills that will be assessed by allowing your child to misbehave, giving the child every excuse you can think of, and by rewarding bad behavior.

Another important skill is to know the difference between what is mine, and what is yours, and that never the twain shall meet without consent. To know that forcing someone to give you something is called bullying and is not OK, and can get your child thrown out of kindergarten, sent to a psychologist and labeled with behavior disorders of many types. Your child may simply be suffering from a family that allows and even models that type of behavior in the home, or neighborhood.

Having spent a large part of my adult career (me Liz) with juvenile criminals and in other criminal rehabilitation projects, I noticed that one trait almost every single criminal had was a disrespect for what belongs to others, including their own bodies. Rape, Maim, Robbery, Murder, Manslaughter, Arson are ALL crimes that require harming others, or touching their bodies or property. IF your child has learned to respect what belongs to others, they are going to avoid being caught and convicted of these crimes. And you will not have to hear my voice saying "I told you so", as the judge says 25 to life, or the coroner shows you your own child.

Some of the criminals have had a history of their own rights being so violated in their home and neighborhood they have no idea of boundaries. While our children need to recognize genocide, and slavery, and trafficking of humans as crimes, and violations of others rights, they also need to recognize how these crimes might have affected their own lives. Whether Grandparents, parents, or even farther back in the family history, many Americans have been victims of these human crimes. It has often been translated to the right to do these things to others. Revenge is a crime in America. And it hurts us, and our children more than having any effect on those who did the bad acts.

It is up to parents to look at their own beliefs and what they are teaching their children. As we say to parents in parenting programs, it is too late when the police come to your door and ask you to come to the coroners office to identify what is left of your child, or as you sit and hear the judge say, tried as a adult, ad 25 to life for what your child has done to someone else's child (no matter what age, everyone is someone's child).

Before age five, grandparents and paid child care can help parents to have a moment for themselves. Parents NEED to figure out what THEIR life is, and how to create a family life that includes those wishes, dreams and NEEDS.

A GOOD parenting class is NEEDED. Most of us did NOT have the best parenting for either our parents, or ourselves. My Mom wanted to finish her career goals. She had not checked out the reality, that when World War II ended, the men came marching home and women were simply expected to go back to the kitchen in their bare feet and plop out a lot of kids so they would be "barefoot and pregnant". Watch some of the series family shows of the fifties and sixties. Dad did not seem to have a real job, even if a doctor or business owner, he had plenty of time to hang around and teach Mom how to run the house and family. Mom, although she had been employed during the war, gone to college, and helped out both sets of aging in-laws was expected to put on cute little aprons over just right house dresses, except for the two or three who always seemed to be wearing haute couture and high heels, probably left over from their careers running businesses because all the men were drafted and sent off to war. Now she could not manage to make a bag lunch of peanut butter sandwich on plain white bread and an apple without Dad's sage advice.

TWO people had a child, today it is impossible to pay rent, mortgage, and all the expenses of running a home without both parents working. This does NOT have to mean two menial jobs. One of the most well paying jobs I had, especially since I did not have to pay child care bills, was licensed critical foster care. I did NOT take foster children, I did day, night and weekend care for doctors, first responders, bus drivers, truck drivers and others who had to either go to work strange hours, or might get caught at work for hours. My younger son hated the after school facility, and said, do something else, so we invented our own licensed care, invited my Aunt to live with us since she did not want to live with her recently married daughters or sons, and we all had a great time being what I called the coolest family on the block.........we used to laugh when we went to the market, or an amusement park or beach, kids of all different ages, and races, calling each other brother and sister, that was their idea, not mine......People gave us some strange looks. Some even dared to ask why I had so many children. Just a lot of twins and triplets I would say, NONE of the kids looked enough alike to be twins.

THE MAJOR point is, TALK to each other, the family and yourself and create a better lifestyle that will sustain all of you. NOT what some magazine, or talk show says you have to do, what you all WANT to do, with a good dose of reality thrown in as a model for your children.

Take a class if needed. There are several online, on You Tube, and in books for the whole family to help each person become part of the whole of a happy, thriving family for all of the members. If it is time for one of the Grandparents, or an old Aunt, or Uncle to come live in, work it out.

This does not mean a vicious, snarling, bell ringing nightmare moves into your home. When my Mother decided she wanted to come live at my home, I said, OK, buy a nice rocking chair, find a good place on the porch, and sit in that chair, and SHUT THE F)()(*k up. She got into the new car my sister had given her, and went on a several months road trip across the United States and Canada, visiting old friends whose children had grown and gone, and/or spouse had divorced or passed, and had a great journey to tell everyone about when she got back and took on her own home once again. IF a person NEEDS too much care, make up your mind, they have to go to a home, and if they do NOT need that much care, they can come, but handle their own life, not strangle the life out of yours, and your children's lives.

Spouses need to make a written contract, each one deals with their own parents, siblings, etc. IF it becomes a problem to the family, the person has a family conference, hire a mediator if necessary and get a written contract about what exactly their living with the family means. YOU do NOT have to give up your life for anyone, not your children, or your in-laws, or your own family members. If a person has strength and mean temperament enough to ring bells, demand services and harm your quality of life, they have enough strength and mean temperament to live alone or in a retirement or nursing facility.

A FIVE year old is NOT competent to run a household, do not let them. Again, take a parenting class. DO NOT let a social worker, or school psychologist tell you that your child CAN NOT behave. Our member Psychiatrists, therapists and teachers have ALL worked with children with severe physical reasons for not learning how to behave, and they LEARN, with kindness, and consistency. ALL of our therapeutic team members have dealt with their professional peers who have taken an attitude that a child with any issue should not be expected to be their best selves, but instead be allowed to "be their diagnosis".

CHAPTER SIX

Age Six to Eleven

The Catch 22 (read the book, or look up the definition in an American language dictionary after the seventies. Joseph Heller, 1961, author of Catch 22)of raising children is that you must have been crazy to want them, but it is even crazier to not want them once you have invest half their lives in loving them.

The next dilemma in raising a child is to raise your child to be themself, NOT what you wished you were at their age.

Children need to survive in the real world, that means YOU need to teach them enough to be able to survive, and even thrive if they choose to in academia, or whatever they choose later on in life, BUT not take childhood away from them.

It may be reality that most of what is taught in school is to pass the tests so the districts can get more money next year, BUT, if your child should decide on a career that requires those pieces of paper, it is up to you to make sure they have an understanding of that reality, In old days children took care of the oxen, the sheep, the buffalo, and cleaned and smoked fish and produce to last over the winter if they wanted to eat during the cold months. Parents taught their children that playing with poison plants, and mountain lions, or hyenas was not likely to allow them to grow up with all their body parts, or to grow up at all.

Children had to learn that if they did not do their job of feeding and watering the farm animals, they died, and the food sources of the family were depleted. They had to learn not to eat ALL the eggs, or there would be no birds to lay eggs and raise new flocks the next year. They had to learn to pick out often poisonous weeds BEFORE harvesting and grinding grains or the whole family and/or their customers could die. Dead customers do NOT buy things. It also is bad for the family reputation to have poisoned their customers.

Today children need to learn, if you want that piece of paper to do what you want in life, you might as well stop fighting it, and learn how to do the rote papers, and pass the rote tests and move on to a place where hopefully they do not just end up the burger flippers of the science, legal and medical fields. This is not to demean burger flippers, they feed millions better food that has been the norm for centuries. Even kings and other leaders often got food poisoning from improperly stored, or prepared food. The thought is, that those who train to be top chefs should not be mandatorily stuck as burger flippers because they do not have five major degrees whimsically required for them to have a restaurant. But, reality is real, and we all have to learn to deal with it, not try to fight it ALL at the wrong time, in the wrong way.

At the same time, your child needs to learn how to pick out good things to learn for what they DO want to do in their lives.

Children during this age period should learn to garden, to relax, to meditate, to pray, to honor something besides the almighty big buck.

CHAPTER SEVEN

Age Twelve to Fourteen

The Catch 22 (read the book, or look up the definition in an American language dictionary after the seventies)of this age is that on the one side, your child needs to begin to take more and more responsibility for their own choices, and lives, and yet…….they need to know you are there (NOT to get them out of trouble) to love them no matter what.

Many parents think this is the time to let their kids go.

It is not.

Yet, it is the time to have completely open communication. My sons were law student kids, and decided themselves early on to have contracts, to negotiate and renegotiate contracts. At this age they were told, you be honest, and tell me what you are wanting to do, you listen carefully to the WHY I do not want you do to some of them, and YOU pay for what you want to do. THEN, if you decide to do it anyway, at least you can call for help. I told them if they did things that ended them up in jail, it was their responsibility. They had not had to come visit me in jail or prison. They did not do without things because I had to pay bail, or lawyers, fees, or fines. They could expect the same. If they were man enough to get into a mess, they better be man enough to get out of it.

I also told them, sex is about one thing, creating new people. IF you create a new person, it is YOUR responsibility. If a girl comes to the door and says she is pregnant, do not open your mouths to say it's not mine. If you choose to hang out with girls with serious mental problems, drug problems and not use birth control, I do NOT want you to whine. I would never make them marry someone, but they would be good fathers. Today we do have DNA, I would sell say, do NOT say I want a DNA test. Boys need to understand that the possibility of creating a human that will suffer is way too important to be taken lightly, use birth control, do not say, "she said she was using the pill".

I was raised by my parents to believe that what is between two people sexually is between those two people, it is not my, or anyone else's business, HOWEVER, if they have a child, it is NOT my or anyone else's business or expense either.

I was also raised to believe that pornography is NOT sex, it is something that makes a huge amount of money using young people to create movies, or video, or magazine pictures to get dirty old men and beat off young boys to buy the materials and the things that go along with those who get addicted to pornography. NONE Of this is about two people who love one another sharing intimacy. If you want to have sex in a bathtub filled with jello, or whipping cream, or dog poop, it is none of my business, as long as you clean it up after yourselves.

I was as open with their girlfriends. I had seen at least one of my foster brothers falsely accused of being responsible for his girlfriend getting pregnant, I knew she just made it up because she thought he would marry her.

My sons had their own phones and from time to time would call and say, HEY MOM, could you get this girl on a ladder away from my window.

We called them "MOM talks" and no matter what time of night, I went out, sat on the porch and talked to young girls about the fact that stalking a boy, and bringing your own ladder to climb into his room whether he had a girl friend or not, or wanted you there at all, was NOT a way to build good self esteem, or a good relationship. Many of those girls are still MY friends over decades. And thank me for a Mom talk their own mothers, or foster Mothers had not had with them.

This is a great time for YOU to think about life goals you may have set aside while your children were small. GO back to school, it is easier than ever as many of the big universities have online classes in almost all subjects. This is a great time to let the family know you are going to start your art, music, or other career back up, and ask for support. The kids are less and less likely to want your full attention every day, and can learn to have empathy for your dreams. It will help them in building relationships to understand not everyone is looking out ONLY for their wants and desires.

Begin to talk to your children at this point about vehicle safety and the responsibility for their own health. Tell them, if you are out with friends, and someone is drunk driving, get out, take a bus, a taxi, or call home for a ride. Go visit some victims of drunk drivers. Ask your children to join SADD or MADD and help make sure others do not get injured by a selfish and immature person.

YOU and your spouse should have long before created a designated driver plan so ONE of you can drink more than one beer, or one wine on special occasions, leaving the other one sober to deal with family emergencies, and drive home safely.

CHAPTER EIGHT

Age Fifteen to Eighteen

The Catch 22 (read the book, or look up the definition in an American language dictionary after the seventies)of this age is again, your child is more and more independent, yet more and more in need of your support and love. NOT bailing them out, but helping them figure it out when they make mistakes.

One day we went to a graduation ceremony for a family youth. He had had a very bad year at his private school (the gangs were so bad no public schools were safe, and his parents gave up a lot to pay for private school to give him a chance for his dreams in life and to live long enough to accomplish them.). as they went through the awards, we paid little attention, and as expected, after that bad year, he did not get any awards. When they got to the highest award for the top achieving student, we did not even pay attention, that surely was not him. BUT to our surprise, it was him. HE had gotten a clear message about his major failure and worked hard to fix his life. He DID have dreams that included college, and he got the message that failing high school was NOT going to get him to his college of choice, or to his dreams.

Hopefully you have already taught your child that "trendy" is a made up ideal for those who cannot live on their own merits. That have to be part of the pack, and try to make believe they are non-conforming and rebels, instead of people wasting their young lives. Often putting their own, and the family lives at risk.

There are programs designed to help families deal with these issues before they become a "model" of failure for their younger siblings. THE PARENT PROJECT is our favorite, it is NOT our program, but can be found online. Local parents and youth professionals get together WITH the youth to change the behavior and outcomes.

Again, this is a great time for parents to be moving ahead with old dreams and plans, or moving careers and dreams ahead rather than blame all their problems on misbehaving youth in the family. If your child needs treatment programs, or special juvenile programs, make sure that they are there, that your child attends, and that the money comes from that youth's efforts, NOT the rest of the family doing with out.

BE truly aware. There is one famous rapper, when he got involved in gangs, his Mother found his guns, and said, either you get out of the gangsta life, or we will leave. He did not, just hid them under the mattress. He came home to find his Mother and the little kids had moved away. He is to be commended for his own courage, he lived in an abandoned car, and finished school while building a rapper career and staying out of the worst of gang activity.

Gang district attorneys have way too many cases of kids who get involved in gangs because they let gang kids hang out while their parents are at work. The parents find out, and say no more, the parents, and often the gangsta wanna be end up dead. This is not dramatic, it is reality.

Drugs, and other addictions are cries for help, they are not trendy behavior. Girls who think they are trendy and doing "cammy' or "sugar daddy" money making scams often end up dead, or sold into sex trafficking. YOUR child NEEDS to know the realities of online scams on young people. One of the gang District Attorneys spoke to a group of private school parents about sex trafficking of stupid rich girls. One of the men had bought a porn film about "private school girls:.. He recognized his daughter's best friend in a video of a party of young girls and rich older men. He was smart enough to figure out if she was doing this, so was his daughter, and went to see the other father. They went to the police. It turned out many young girls from that posh girls school thought they were all that, they did not even get paid…….they got to ride in a limo, and drink champagne and after a few drinks and some drugs, given some sexy lingerie. They were shocked to find out it was all paid for by the nasty old men who were child molesters, AND the sale of the videos. TALK TO YOUR KIDS, they need to know reality.

CHAPTER NINE

College, Marriage, Career, Grandchildren Addictions, Disability, Picking Up The Pieces

The Catch 22 (read the book, or look up the definition in an American language dictionary after the seventies) of your children growing up is that they need you and the family more at this time than any other, and often are too arrogant, or too proud to ask for the help they need if they have not been raised to believe that family is supportive, not trying to take over their lives, or prove they are losers and NEED help to exist.

COLLEGE: College is NOT a requirement for all people. There are many online programs, especially those offered as extension courses by many colleges and universities and technological institutes where both you and your child are able to learn about the subjects and how to use those subjects in your own life and career.

HOWEVER, all children NEED to be ready for college should they decide a science or academic career is something they would like to pursue.

A GED while it allows a person who has not completed high school to catch up on "things" of learning, will NOT fill in the in class conversations, discussions, and seminars that train a student to look at learning in a new way. NONE of us is RIGHT. Even scientists teach that there is only ONE truth in science, and that truth is that everything changes and as we learn things, what we once thought was true, is not, just as the world is not flat!!! Once something every person believed.

Think for instance back to the chapter on Math. Some people might say that one and one are two, that is absolute and the TRUTH. In fact, if you do not know what each of those ones are, you do NOT know that one and one are two. If you have one canary and one cat, you soon have one fat cat if the cat figures out how to get to that canary. One cake and one child may equal one fat, sick child, and a messed up cake. OR it may equal a very sick child if the cake has things in it the child is allergic to and has eaten. The purpose of college is to teach a person new things, how to discuss and examine those things, and how to form their own opinions, whether right or wrong. AND that right and wrong can be subjective. This is called "critical thinking" and is one of the major purposes of college. A Masters Degree is to learn what research has been done in the area you are working with, and how to use that material, as well as how to find out if it is reliable material or not. A PhD is original research, and is supposed to train a person to think beyond what is there, and document it scientifically and legally. While. PhD can be successful if the research shows the researcher is RIGHT, a person also learns that sometimes research that proves themselves to be WRONG can be equally, or often MORE useful than just always being "right". Graduate school is supposed to teach the student to look at what is there, to ask what

COULD be there, and do research to see what happens, no matter the outcome being their vision, or not.

DO NOT RUN IN THE HALLWAYS might be changed if there is a fire. YET, the worst thing a group of people can do is to run in a mob if there is a threat, they are likely to injure and kill more persons by the running and knocking down of others, and trampling them, than would have been the reality if they had ALL exited in a helpful and cautious way. IF someone yells "fire" and everyone runs out, and in fact there is a mass shooter outside the door, that running is definitely the wrong thing to do. Learning the rules, and how and when to apply or change them is a big part of college.

MARRIAGE and relationships

Parents NEED to teach their children that NO ONE needs a romantic relationship as a child, and certainly NO CHILD needs to have sex. A shocking reality in America today is that there are NINE year old mothers. The two here in Los Angeles both were continuously raped by their Mother's boyfriend. The Mothers knew. When questioned, they said they did not stand up for their child because then the boyfriend would not pay the rent.

Pimping out your eight year old is a felony and will get both Mother and her boyfriend (or girlfriend) in prison, and registered as sexual predators, and child molesters on the registered sex offender mandatory lifetime parole lists.

Many people are immigrating from other countries, or a certain State, believe it is OK for an adult male to "marry" an eleven year old child. They are shocked when they are arrested and tried as child molesters and sentenced to prison, and then put on the sexual predator offender lists on lifetime parole. The parents of the girls are often arrested and convicted of child abuse as well. What has been a well respected tradition in "the old country" is a crime in America. Many countries have had centuries of tradition of giving up their daughters, either as wives, or concubines to rich men, for payment of animals, land, and money. In America pimping out your daughters (or sons) is illegal and punishable by prison time, or being deported as felons. or both.

America gives freedom OF a choice of religion, NOT a freedom to use religion as an excuse to commit felonies and harm other persons lives, especially children.

Many people believe parents have a right to tell their children WHO to marry. America gives every person the RIGHT to marry, or not as they decide as adults. Parents need to learn the laws, and give their children the rights they themselves came to America to obtain.

Many children, teens and college age persons believe they have a RIGHT to money or inheritance from their parents. Many believe their parents owe them a college education. Many children, teens, and college age persons believe their parents OWE them a dowery, or marriage gift of large amounts of money and/or real estate. This is NOT true in America. Teach your children to be grateful for what they are given, and not to EXPECT or DEMAND things, it will harm them as adults who feel they are entitled and become very disliked for this behavior.

With freedom, comes responsibility, and possibly a loss of "duties" of both parents and children. It is important to discuss these issues with your family and not alienate love and care of either children or parents with arguments and divisions that are not realistic, or in many cases legal in America.

How does all this relate to sex? Sex is the creation of a new human and the responsibility for that human. Psalms 37:10 says that even if the flesh and blood parents abandon (or die, or are sold off for slaves in those days) the Creator of ALL is still here for us and will never abandon us.

Whatever pornography, personal antics, or family driven ideas of sexuality exist, they are something, generally labeled sex, but these realities need to be discussed with your children at age appropriate times as good parents.

CHAPTER TEN

Human Sexuality for All Ages of Children

The Catch 22 (read the book, or look up the definition in an American language dictionary after the seventies) of teaching your child human sexuality is trying to figure out how to teach them sexuality is normal, and healthy, yet at the same time teaching them the responsibility, and the pit falls of sexuality.

Leaving the teaching of sexuality to others, their peers, the school, or the internet and movies or pornography is NOT going to work out well.

The most important ingredient of teaching your child(ren) appropriate human sexuality is to figure out your own issues with human sexuality many years before the questions arise.

There is a joke, in which a young person comes in and asks the parent, "where did I come from". The parent has long prepared for this dreaded question. Taken classes, bought books and video for each age level. When the question arose, the parent is well prepared and begins to read the books, and show the videos, and talk to the child. At the end, the parent asks if there is any question the child has. The child replies, yeah, how come Joey came from Texas, and I needed to learn all this to find out where I was born.

This joke reminds us to ASK our children what they are asking. ASK our children what they are needing.

A child on a farm grows up knowing that baby chicks grow in eggs, and are born and grow into chickens. A child in the city has asked how the grocery store gets the egg inside those"plastic" containers and seals them.

And yet, a woman wrote to a newspaper columnist and said, I see no reason for sex education, I grew up on a horse ranch and learned all I need to know from watching the horses breed. The columnist drily replied that the woman must have found her husband sadly shortchanged when the wedding night came.

Today's children, for the most part, wonder why people wait until the wedding night, they say they would not buy a car they had not tried out. We can NOT make our children be what we are waiting for them to ask to give us a chance to be the perfect parents in raising balanced and self assessing sexual humans.

We have to ASK them what they need to know.

It is important for you to teach your child about the real world about them if you expect, or hope that one day they may be successful should they want a career in science, technology, agriculture, architecture, engineering or manufacturing at any level beyond hard labor, or mindless assembly positions.

Sex is a very big part of our lives. It is used to sell everything from pizza to cars, to underarm deodorant, and every other item on sale. We even see senior incontinence supplies sold showing men and women in good looking clothing, or swimming in swim wear rather than nice old folks who just can not make it to the bathroom in time.

Children NEED to know what sex really is. They need to know that a woman in a bikini with a pouty kissy face has absolutely NOTHING to do with buying a car. They need to know that a woman has every right to wear that bikini to the market if she wants to and not be bothered by anyone. for any reason. They need to know that in fact, men do NOT think about or need sex every three minutes. The backroom jocks may, but most men have more interesting things and more important things on their minds, such as taking care of their children, spouses and homes, and aging parents, white river rafting, mountain bike riding, fixing their motorcycle and polishing up the car to get to the job that pays for things needed, or to the career that pays for it all and is exciting and part of who each man should be. Every man his to learn to live peacefully and successfully with his spouse for the benefit of the children and the betterment of the community. Even the most divided of gender societies in the ancient Bible expect a man to take care of the spouse, family and animals and farms to support their lifestyle. Even slaves of those ancient days were expected to also take care of the moral, ethical and education needs of their family.

Sex IS reproduction. Worms and many species of virus and bacteria do not even need a mate to reproduce. There are many species of insects and reptiles, and fish that can be either the male or female. Sea horses, sea dragons and some other species have pouches and the male takes care of the eggs and watches over the smallest fry to preserve their species while Mom has gone off to find another male to pocket more of her eggs.

Except for those species that reproduce without a partner, sex is a sperm and egg that meet and start a new life. This is NOT a religious discussion or dispute over abortion, OR a legal discussion over when life legally begins. It IS an educational guide for parents to make sure their children know what sex is, and how it affects all of us. It IS an educational guide for parents to make sure they know what THEY are talking about before they start teaching their child about human sexuality.

Children need to know that sex creates responsibility. The choice to be a good parent, or not, and how that is defined, in America, and many other countries with equal rights and freedom of religion is the choice of the parent. A father can be a horrible parent, someone who turns his back on his offspring, with no thought as to how their life turns out. This is not about whether a Mother or Father is to blame, it is about, responsibility.

In America the "family" is not the less than 5% cited on the last census as being children living with both their birth parents in one home. Many children live in group homes, are sent to private schools most of the year, or live with relatives, one parent, or one parent and a new spouse, and often children live in adopted, or foster homes. Many children live in homes with two Fathers, or two Mothers. Many more children live in homes with aunts, uncles, and grandparents.

In America, FREEDOM OF RELIGION makes it the RIGHT of every family to pick their own religion, or choose not to have a religion, and it is NOT the duty of one or more groups of those who feel their religion is the ONE religion to make life miserable for the children living in religions of other faiths, or no religion. Parents choose the religion of a family, and it is NOT OK to bully children for any reason, but especially not in "love" for their immortal soul.

This has a very important impact on human sexuality.

People come from other countries with religious backed beliefs as to parents, and how women and girls in particular, are expected to behave, or be punished by any "righteous" person they have the misfortune to meet along the way.

THESE religious issues are NOT valid in America. Many of them amount to child abuse, and/or child molesting.

MOST of these beliefs are ignorant and not based on any reality, either moral, or scientific. In some countries men have raped new born babies of poor people because they thought that if they had sex with a "virgin" they would put their HIV or active AIDS on the victim of the rape, and be free of the disease. Of course that is a stupid and ignorant superstition with not one iota of scientific support. AND, it is a felony in America that comes with a lifetime of being a registered child molester and sex offender.

Many countries believe that a man can have a clean and pure wife, and as many sort of wives (often called concubines) on the side. Other countries allow this practice, but only if the religious leaders say the man can afford more children and to support the concubine for the rest of her life.

Many countries believe that any woman not out in public covered with black or purple clothing so not one peek of her body from head to foot can be seen, is a prostitute and out looking for customers, or to be raped since she is a disrespected person, with no rights. A doctor on a hot day over triple digits was driving from one hospital to another with the windows open due to the heat, she was blocked, her car windows broken, and dragged out and raped and stoned to death because the arm of her robe had blown up and someone saw her forearm and got together a mob. In America this group would be arrested and charged with rape and murder and after serving time in prison would be lifetime registered sex offenders. In recent years a group of men on a bus raped some young school girls, the girls were tried and found guilty of sexually harassing the men and having sex with them illegally and immorally which in those countries is punished by stoning to death. In America the MEN would be considered rapists, child molesters, and after serving prison time as convicted felons, would be lifetime registered sex offenders and pedophiles.

Many men in America today and in the past few years have been arrested and charged with rape, and sexual assault, and/or sexual harassment, as well as had huge money damages awarded in the civil suits because they believed that men just have some kind of right to have sex the way and when they want it. Today women are beginning to be charged and sued for similar offenses. Both men and women are being arrested and sued for offenses against same sex persons as well. AND many men (soon probably women as well) are being charged on what may be, or what may NOT be legitimate claims from way in the past. If we throw out our just systems of law, we better realize one day we might be the one being targeted and arrested or accused of things that may, or may not have happened long ago, long past the statute of limitations. AND we need to make sure people get proper help AT THE TIME of any complaint so justice, not political games is served. This is to take violent criminals off the streets and to protect children NOT to play political games years later.

Athletes and celebrities have begun to carry not just condoms, but legal papers to be signed by any sexual partner, giving legal consent prior to having sex with anyone. I wonder, when does the public notary become involved??? And will there be new nightly open public notaries in hotels, and bars?

Kids Anonymous. KJr.

CHAPTER TWELVE

Closing and Other Books by Author and team

Closing:

All of our group of books, and workbooks contain some work pages, and/or suggestions for the reader, and those teaching these books to make notes, to go to computer, and libraries and ask others for information to help these projects work their best.

To utilize these to their fullest, make sure YOU model the increased thoughts and availability of more knowledge to anyone you share these books and workbooks with in classes, or community groups.

Magazines are, as noted in most of the books, a wonderful place to look for and find ongoing research and information. Online search engines often bring up new research in the areas, and newly published material.

We all have examples of how we learned and who it was that taught us.

One of the strangest lessons I have learned was walking to a shoot in downtown Los Angeles. The person who kindly told me to park my truck in Pasadena, and take the train had been unaware that the weekend busses did NOT run early in the morning when the crews had to be in to set up. That person, being just a participant, was going much later in the day, taking a taxi, and had no idea how often crews do NOT carry purses with credit cards, large amounts of cash, and have nowhere to carry those items, because the crew works hard, and fast during a set up and tear down and after the shoot are TIRED and not looking to have to find items that have been left around, or stolen.

As I walked, I had to travel through an area of Los Angeles that had become truly run down and many homeless were encamped about and sleeping on the sidewalks and in alleys. I saw a man, that having worked in an ER for many years I realized was DEAD. I used to have thoughts about people who did not notice people needing help, I thought, this poor man, this is probably the most peace he has had in a long time. I prayed for him and went off to my unwanted walk across town. As I walked, I thought about myself, was I just heartless, or was I truly thinking this was the only moment of peace this man had had for a long time and just leaving him to it. What good were upset neighbors, and police, fire trucks and ambulances going to do. He was calmly, eyes open, staring out at a world that had failed him while alive, why rush to disturb him now that nothing could be done.

I did make sure he was DEAD. He was, quite cold rigid.

I learned that day that it is best to do what a person needs, NOT what we need.

Learning is about introspection and grounding of material. Passing little tests on short term memory skills and not knowing what it all means is NOT education, or teaching.

As a high school student, in accelerated Math and Science programs, in which I received 4.0 grades consistently, I walked across a field, diagonally, and suddenly all that math and science made sense, it was not just exercises on paper I could throw answers back on paper, but I realized had NO clue as to what it all really meant.

OTHER BOOKS BY THIS AUTHOR, AND TEAM

Most, if not all, of these books are written at a fourth grade level. FIrst, the author is severely brain damaged from a high fever disease caused by a sample that came in the mail, without a warning that it had killed during test marketing. During the law suit, it was discovered that the corporation had known prior to mailing out ten million samples, WITHOUT warnings of disease and known deaths, and then NOT telling anyone after a large number of deaths around the world started. Second, the target audience is high risk youth, and young veterans, most with a poor education before signing into, or being drafted into the military as a hope Many of our veterans are Vietnam or WWII era.

Maybe those recruiting promises would come true. They would be trained, educated, and given chance for a home, and to protect our country and its principles. Watch the movies Platoon, and Born on the Fourth of July as well as the Oliver Stone series on history to find out how these dreams were meet.

DO NOT bother to write and tell us of grammar or spelling errors. We often wrote these books and workbooks fast for copyrights. We had learned our lessons about giving our material away when one huge charity asked us for our material, promising a grant, Instead, we heard a couple of years later they had built their own VERY similar project, except theirs charged for services, ours were FREE, and theirs was just for a small group, ours was training veterans and others to spread the programs as fast as they could.. They got a Nobel Peace prize. We keep saying we are not bitter, we keep saying we did not do our work to get awards, or thousands of dollars of grants....but, it hurts. Especially when lied to and that group STILL sends people to US for help when they can not meet the needs, or the veterans and family can not afford their "charitable" services. One other group had the nerve to send us a Cease and Desist using our own name. We said go ahead and sue, we have proof of legal use of this name for decades. That man had the conscience to apologize, his program was not even FOR veterans or first responders, or their families, nor high risk kids. But we learned. Sometimes life is very unfair.

We got sued again later for the same issue. We settled out of Court as our programs were just restarting and one of the veterans said, let's just change that part of the name and keep on training veterans to run their own programs. Smart young man.

Book List:

DRAGON KITES and other stories:

The Grandparents Story list will add 12 new titles this year. We encourage every family to write their own historic stories. That strange old Aunt who when you listen to her stories left a rich and well regulated life in the Eastern New York coastal fashionable families to learn Telegraph messaging and go out to the old west to LIVE her life. That old Grandfather or Grandmother who was sent by family in other countries torn by war to pick up those "dollars in the streets" as noted in the book of that title.

Books in publication, or out by summer 2021

Carousel Horse: A Children's book about equine therapy and what schools MIGHT be and are in special private programs.

Carousel Horse: A smaller version of the original Carousel Horse, both contain the workbooks and the screenplays used for on site stable programs as well as lock down programs where the children and teens are not able to go out to the stables.

Spirit Horse II: This is the work book for training veterans and others interested in starting their own Equine Therapy based programs. To be used as primary education sites, or for supplementing public or private school programs. One major goal of this book is to copyright our founding material, as we gave it away freely to those who said they wanted to help us get grants. They did not. Instead they built their own programs, with grant money, and with donations in small, beautiful stables and won….a Nobel Peace Prize for programs we invented. We learned our lessons, although we do not do our work for awards, or grants, we DO not like to be ripped off, so now we copyright.

Reassessing and Restructuring Public Agencies; This book is an over view of our government systems and how they were expected to be utilized for public betterment. This is a Fourth Grade level condemnation of a PhD dissertation that was not accepted be because the mentor thought it was "against government" .. The first paragraph noted that a request had been made, and referrals given by the then White House.

Reassessing and Restructuring Public Agencies; TWO. This book is a suggestive and creative work to give THE PEOPLE the idea of taking back their government and making the money spent and the agencies running SERVE the PEOPLE ;not politicians. This is NOT against government, it is about the DUTY of the PEOPLE to oversee and control government before it overcomes us.

Could This Be Magic? A Very Short Book. This is a very short book of pictures and the author's personal experiences as the Hall of Fame band VAN HALEN practiced in her garage. The pictures are taken by the author, and her then five year old son. People wanted copies of the pictures, and permission was given to publish them to raise money for treatment and long term Veteran homes.

Carousel TWO: Equine therapy for Veterans. publication pending 2021

Carousel THREE: Still Spinning: Special Equine therapy for women veterans and single mothers. This book includes TWELVE STEPS BACK FROM BETRAYAL for soldiers who have been sexually assaulted in the active duty military and help from each other to heal, no matter how horrible the situation. publication pending 2021

LEGAL ETHICS: AN OXYMORON. A book to give to lawyers and judges you feel have not gotten the justice of American Constitution based law (Politicians are great persons to gift with this book). Publication late 2021

PARENTS CAN LIVE and raise great kids.

Included in this book are excerpts from our workbooks from KIDS ANONYMOUS and KIDS JR, and A PARENTS PLAIN RAP (to teach sexuality and relationships to their children. This program came from a copyrighted project thirty years ago, which has been networked into our other programs. This is our training work book. We asked AA what we had to do to become a real Twelve Step program as this is considered a quasi twelve step program children and teens can use to heal BEFORE becoming involved in drugs, sexual addiction, sexual trafficking and relationship woes, as well as unwanted, neglected and abused or having children murdered by parents not able to deal with the reality of parenting. Many of our original students were children of abuse and neglect, no matter how wealthy. Often the neglect was by society itself when children lost parents to illness, accidents or addiction. We were told, send us a copy and make sure you call it quasi. The Teens in the first programs when surveyed for the outcome research reports said, WE NEEDED THIS EARLIER. SO they helped younger children invent KIDS JR. Will be republished in 2021 as a documentary of the work and success of these projects.

Addicted To Dick. This is a quasi Twelve Step program for women in domestic violence programs mandated by Courts due to repeated incidents and danger, or actual injury or death of their children.

Addicted to Dick 2018 This book is a specially requested workbook for women in custody, or out on probation for abuse to their children, either by themselves or their sexual partners or spouses. The estimated national number for children at risk at the time of request was three million across the nation. During Covid it is estimated that number has risen. Homelessness and undocumented families that are unlikely to be reported or found are creating discussion of a much larger number of children maimed or killed in these domestic violence crimes. THE most important point in this book is to force every local school district to train teachers, and all staff to recognize children at risk, and to report their family for HELP, not punishment. The second most important part is to teach every child on American soil to know to ask for help, no matter that parents, or other relatives or known adults, or unknown adults have threatened to kill them for "telling". Most, if not all paramedics, emergency rooms, and police and fire stations are trained to protect the children and teens, and get help for the family.. PUNISHMENT is not the goal, eliminating childhood abuse and injury or death at the hands of family is the goal of all these projects. In some areas JUDGES of child and family courts were taking training and teaching programs themselves to HELP. FREE..

Addicted to Locker Room BS. This book is about MEN who are addicted to the lies told in locker rooms and bars. During volunteer work at just one of several huge juvenile lock downs, where juveniles who have been convicted as adults, but are waiting for their 18th birthday to be sent to adult prisons, we noticed that the young boys and teens had "big" ideas of themselves, learned in locker rooms and back alleys. Hundreds of these young boys would march, monotonously around the enclosures, their lives over. often facing long term adult prison sentences.

The girls, we noticed that the girls, for the most part were smart, had done well in school, then "something" happened. During the years involved in this volunteer work I saw only ONE young girl who was so mentally ill I felt she was not reachable, and should be in a locked down mental health facility for help; if at all possible, and if teachers, and others had been properly trained, helped BEFORE she gotten to that place, lost in the horror and broken of her childhood and early teen years.

We noticed that many of the young women in non military sexual assault healing programs were "betrayed" in many ways, by step fathers, boyfriends, even fathers, and mothers by either molestation by family members, or allowing family members or friends of parents to molest these young women, often as small children. We asked military sexually assaulted young women to begin to volunteer to help in the programs to heal the young girls and teens, it helped heal them all.

There was NOTHING for the boys that even began to reach them until our research began on the locker room BS theory of life destruction and possible salvaging by the boys themselves, and men in prisons who helped put together something they thought they MIGHT have heard before they ended up in prison.

Americans CAN Live Happily Ever After. Parents edition.One

Americans CAN Live Happily Ever After. Children's edition Two.

Americans CAN Live Happily Ever After. Three. After Covid. This book includes "Welcome to America" a requested consult workbook for children and youth finding themselves in cages, auditoriums on cots, or in foster group homes or foster care of relatives or non-relatives with NO guidelines for their particular issues. WE ASKED the kids, and they helped us write this fourth grade level workbook portion of this book to help one another and each other. Written in a hurry! We were asked to use our expertise in other youth programs, and our years of experience teaching and working in high risk youth programs to find something to help.

REZ CHEESE Written by a Native American /WASP mix woman. Using food, and thoughts on not getting THE DIABETES, stories are included of a childhood between two worlds.

REZ CHEESE TWO A continuation of the stress on THE DIABETES needing treatment and health care from birth as well as recipes, and stories from Native America, including thoughts on asking youth to help stop the overwhelming numbers of suicide by our people.

BIG LIZ: LEADER OF THE GANG Stories of unique Racial Tension and Gang Abatement projects created when gangs and racial problems began to make schools unsafe for our children.

DOLLARS IN THE STREETS, ghost edited for author Lydia Caceras, the first woman horse trainer at Belmont Park.

95 YEARS of TEACHING:

A book on teaching, as opposed to kid flipping

Two teachers who have created and implemented systems for private and public education a combined 95 plus years of teaching talk about experiences and realities and how parents can get involved in education for their children. Included are excerpts from our KIDS ANONYMOUS and KIDS JR workbooks of over 30 years of free youth programs.

A HORSE IS NOT A BICYCLE. A book about pet ownership and how to prepare your children for responsible pet ownership and along the way to be responsible parents. NO ONE needs to own a pet, or have a child, but if they make that choice, the animal, or child deserves a solid, caring forever home.

OLD MAN THINGS and MARE'S TALES. this is a fun book about old horse trainers I met along the way. My husband used to call the old man stories "old man things", which are those enchanting and often very effective methods of horse, pet, and even child rearing. I always said I brought up my children and my students the same as I had trained horses and dogs......I meant that horses and dogs had taught me a lot of sensible, humane ways to bring up an individual, caring, and dream realizing adult who was HAPPY and loved.

STOP TALKING, DO IT

ALL of us have dreams, intentions, make promises. This book is a workbook from one of our programs to help a person make their dreams come true, to build their intentions into goals, and realities, and to keep their promises. One story from this book, that inspired the concept is a high school kid, now in his sixties, that was in a special ed program for drug abuse and not doing well in school. When asked, he said his problem was that his parents would not allow him to buy a motorcycle. He admitted that he did not have money to buy one, insure one, take proper driver's education and licensing examinations to own one, even though he had a job. He was asked to figure out how much money he was spending on drugs. Wasting his own money, stealing from his parents and other relatives, and then to figure out, if he saved his own money, did some side jobs for neighbors and family until he was 18, he COULD afford the motorcycle and all it required to legally own one. In fact, he did all, but decided to spend the money on college instead of the motorcycle when he graduated from high school. His priorities had changed as he learned about responsible motorcycle ownership and risk doing the assignments needed for his special ed program. He also gave up drugs, since his stated reason was he could not have a motorcycle, and that was no longer true, he COULD have a motorcycle, just had to buy it himself, not just expect his parents to give it to him.

Printed in the United States
by Baker & Taylor Publisher Services